FTU

JOHANNES BRAHMS

Complete Chamber Music for Strings and Clarinet Quintet

EDITED BY HANS GÁL

THE VIENNA GESELLSCHAFT DER MUSIKFREUNDE EDITION

———

33092

Dover Publications, Inc., New York

Contents

Published in Canada by General Publishing Company, Ltd.,
30 Lesmill Road, Don Mills, Toronto, Ontario.

This Dover edition, first published in 1968, is an unabridged
republication of Volume (*Band*) 7, entitled *Kammermusik für
Streichinstrumente*, of the collection *Johannes Brahms; Sämtliche
Werke; Ausgabe der Gesellschaft der Musikfreunde in Wien*, originally
published by Breitkopf & Härtel, Leipzig (n.d.; Editor's Preface to
Volume 7 dated Spring, 1927).
The English translation of the Editor's Preface (*Revisionsbericht*)
and of the table of contents was prepared especially
for this Dover edition.

Standard Book Number: 486-21914-3
Library of Congress Catalog Card Number: 68–11722
Manufactured in the United States of America
Dover Publications, Inc.
180 Varick Street
New York, N.Y. 10014

EDITOR'S PREFACE

SEXTET NO. 1, OP. 18.

BASIC TEXTS FOR THE PRESENT EDITION:

1. The score edition published by Simrock.
2. Brahms's personal copy of the score, in the collection of the Gesellschaft der Musikfreunde, Vienna.
3. The edition in parts.

COMMENTS:

The work was published in 1862 by N. Simrock, Berlin, with the title: "Sextett für 2 Violinen, 2 Violen und 2 Violoncelli componirt von Johannes Brahms. Op. 18." Publication number 6202.

Except for insignificant oversights (performance indications missing in individual parts, and similar items) the score as well as the parts are free of errors. Brahms's personal copy contains only one correction, an e♮ in Violin I in measure 379 of the last movement.

In measures 192 and 215 of the last movement Viola I also has the notes of Viola II, forming double stops; these additional notes, out of place in both instances, have been deleted. In measure 334 of the last movement both violas have b♭ instead of a.

SEXTET NO. 2, OP. 36.

BASIC TEXTS FOR THE PRESENT EDITION:

1. The score edition published by Simrock.
2. Brahms's personal copy of the score, in the collection of the Gesellschaft der Musikfreunde, Vienna.
3. The edition in parts.

COMMENTS:

The second sextet was published in 1866 by N. Simrock, Berlin, with the title: "Sextett für 2 Violinen, 2 Violen und 2 Violoncelli componirt von Johannes Brahms. Op. 36." Publication number 6474.

The score contains a number of insignificant engraving errors, some of which are noted in the personal copy, while the parts are practically free of errors. The personal copy also contains other notations referring to performance; these changes, taken into account in this edition, are as follows:

The tempo of the third movement originally read "Poco adagio." The long *crescendo* and *descrescendo* signs in measures 1–4 are later additions.

The *marcato* signs (>) in the opening theme of the last movement (measure 1, fourth and seventh eighth notes) are added in the personal copy everywhere the theme appears, as are the analogous *sforzati* in the coda (measures 147 ff., 167 ff.). In measures 7–11 of this movement Violin I originally had no *legato* slurs. The somewhat inconsistent phrasings of this theme were also rectified in the further course of the movement in accordance with the slurs drawn in at the beginning.

QUINTET NO. 1, OP. 88.

BASIC TEXTS FOR THE PRESENT EDITION:

1. The score edition published by Simrock.
2. Brahms's personal copy of the score, in the collection of the Gesellschaft der Musikfreunde, Vienna.

COMMENTS:

This quintet was published in 1883 by N. Simrock, Berlin, with the title: "Quintett für zwei Violinen, zwei Bratschen und Violoncell von Johannes Brahms. Op. 88." Publication number 8314.

The score is nearly flawless. The only change in the personal copy is the insertion of a missing ◁▷ in Violin I in measure 203 of the second movement. In the first movement, measure 139, the third quarter note of Viola I reads ; this was rectified to correspond to measure 143. Similarly, in measure 108 of the second movement the fourth eighth note of Viola I, which was d♯, has been corrected to correspond to measure 24 of the movement. Moreover, an obvious error needed to be corrected in measure 87 of the last movement: in the last quarter of this measure Viola I has the chord

This chord cannot be played on the viola; we have therefore deleted the highest note, which can be done without since it is contained in the Viola II part anyway.

QUINTET NO. 2, OP. 111.

BASIC TEXTS FOR THE PRESENT EDITION:

1. The score edition published by Simrock.
2. Brahms's personal copy of the score, in the collection of the Gesellschaft der Musikfreunde, Vienna.

COMMENTS:

The work was published in 1891 with the title: "Zweites Quintett (G dur) für zwei Violinen, zwei Bratschen und Violoncell von Johannes Brahms. Op 111." Publication number 9508.

The score is nearly flawless; the personal copy shows no corrections.

QUINTET, OP. 115.

BASIC TEXTS FOR THE PRESENT EDITION:

1. The score edition published by Simrock.
2. The edition in parts published by Simrock.
3. Brahms's personal copy of the score, in the collection of the Gesellschaft der Musikfreunde, Vienna.
4. The original manuscript, in the collection of the Gesellschaft der Musikfreunde, Vienna.

COMMENTS:

The work was published in 1892 by N. Simrock, Berlin, with the title: "Quintett für Clarinette (oder Bratsche) 2 Violinen, Bratsche und Violoncell von Johannes Brahms. Op. 115." Publication number 9710. The score is practically free of errors; a few insignificant inaccuracies (in slurs and such matters) were corrected in accordance with the edition in parts. The personal copy contains a correction which had to be reckoned with here: in the original edition the fifth variation in the last movement (measure 161) has the tempo indication "Con moto," which seems to be modified by the indication "Un poco meno mosso" in the coda, measure 193. In the personal copy both indications are crossed out; this expresses clearly Brahms's desire for a uniform tempo throughout the movement (𝅗𝅥 = 𝅗𝅥), a tempo that agrees exactly with that of the first movement, the principal theme of which recurs in this coda.

At the end of the original manuscript is the date: "Ischl. Sommer 91. J. B." The manuscript contains a noteworthy variant, projected at some later date and sketched in only hastily; this is an alteration and expansion of the principal subject of the first movement which heightens the effect of this passage incomparably. In the manuscript, measures 10 ff. still read as follows:

QUARTETS NO. 1 AND NO. 2, OP. 51.

BASIC TEXTS FOR THE PRESENT EDITION:
1. The score edition published by N. Simrock, Berlin.
2. The edition in parts, same publisher.
3. Brahms's personal copy of the score, in the collection of the Gesellschaft der Musikfreunde, Vienna.
4. The original manuscripts of both quartets, in the collection of the Gesellschaft der Musikfreunde, Vienna.

COMMENTS:

The quartets were published (in individual editions) in 1873 by N. Simrock with the title: "Zwei Quartette für 2 Violinen, Bratsche und Violoncell, seinem Freunde Dr. Theodor Billroth in Wien zugeeignet von Johannes Brahms. Op. 51. No. 1. C moll. No. 2. A moll." Publication numbers 7378 and 7379.

Score and parts are nearly flawless. The personal copy of the C minor quartet has no entry, that of the A minor quartet has a correction of an engraving error (third movement, measure 173, raised to *d♯* in Violin I) and a small change in the Violin I part in measures 21 and 22 of the last movement, which in the original edition read as follows:

A comparison with the (undated) original manuscripts yielded nothing significant for this edition.

QUARTET NO. 3, OP. 67.

BASIC TEXTS FOR THE PRESENT EDITION:
1. The score edition published by Simrock.
2. The edition in parts published by Simrock.

3. Brahms's personal copy of the score, in the collection of the Gesellschaft der Musikfreunde, Vienna.
4. The original manuscript (privately owned).

COMMENTS:

This quartet was published in 1876 by N. Simrock, Berlin, with the title: "Quartett (in B dur No. 3) für 2 Violinen, Bratsche und Violoncell, seinem Freunde Professor Th. W. Engelmann in Utrecht zugeeignet von Johannes Brahms. Op. 67." Publication number 7892.

The score and the parts editions are both practically free of errors. The personal copy contains a few slight alterations, which were taken into account here. The original readings follow:

Second movement, measure 36; on the last quarter note Violin I originally had:

The same rhythm originally occurred in measures 38 and 39 of the Violin II part. (The change results in regular thirty-seconds instead of thirty-second-note triplets.)

Third movement, measure 103; the last eighth note in Violin I was *e* instead of *g*. In the coda of this movement, measures 193 and 194, the viola had the following:

The original manuscript shows numerous later alterations, the most interesting of which involves measures 172–178 of the last movement. In place of these seven measures there originally occurred the following nine:

Vienna
Spring, 1927

Hans Gál

SEXTETT NR. 1, OP. 18.

VORLAGEN:

1. Die Simrocksche Partiturausgabe.
2. Brahms' Handexemplar der Partitur, im Besitz der Gesellschaft der Musikfreunde in Wien.
3. Die Stimmenausgabe.

BEMERKUNGEN:

Das Werk erschien im Jahre 1862 bei N. Simrock in Berlin, mit dem Titel: »Sextett für 2 Violinen, 2 Violen und 2 Violoncelli componirt von Johannes Brahms. Op. 18.« Verlagsnummer 6202.

Die Partitur ist bis auf unwesentliche Flüchtigkeiten (in einzelnen Stimmen fehlende Vortragszeichen u. dgl.) fehlerfrei, ebenso die Stimmen. Brahms' Handexemplar enthält eine einzige Korrektur, nämlich im 379. Takt des Finales ein ♮e in der 1. Violine.

Takt 192 und Takt 215 des Finales stehen in der 1. Bratsche, als Doppelgriffe, auch die Noten der 2. Bratsche, die, da jedenfalls irrtümlich, beseitigt wurden. Takt 334 des Finales steht in beiden Bratschen b anstatt a.

SEXTETT NR. 2, OP. 36.

VORLAGEN:

1. Die Simrocksche Partiturausgabe.
2. Brahms' Handexemplar der Partitur, im Besitz der Gesellschaft der Musikfreunde in Wien.
3. Die Stimmenausgabe.

BEMERKUNGEN:

Das 2. Sextett erschien im Jahre 1866 bei N. Simrock in Berlin, mit dem Titel: »Sextett für 2 Violinen, 2 Violen und 2 Violoncelli componirt von Johannes Brahms. Op. 36.« Verlagsnummer 6474.

Die Partitur enthält eine Anzahl unwesentlicher Stichfehler, die zum Teil im Handexemplar angemerkt sind, während die Stimmen fast fehlerlos sind. Das Handexemplar enthält auch sonst Anmerkungen, die sich auf den Vortrag beziehen und hier berücksichtigt wurden. Diese Änderungen sind nachstehend angeführt.

Das Tempo des 3. Satzes lautete ursprünglich Poco adagio. Die langen Crescendo- und Decrescendogabeln im 1.—4. Takt sind nachträglich hinzugesetzt.

Die Marcatozeichen (>) im Anfangsthema des letzten Satzes (Takt 1, 4. und 7. Achtel) sind überall, wo das Thema erscheint, im Handexemplar hinzugesetzt, in der Koda im gleichen Sinn Sforzati (Takt 147 ff., Takt 167 ff.). Takt 7—11 des Finales war die 1. Violine ursprünglich ohne Legatobogen. Die einigermaßen inkonsequenten Phrasierungen dieses Themas wurden auch im weiteren Verlauf des Satzes im Sinne der dort eingetragenen Bogenbezeichnung richtiggestellt.

QUINTETT NR. 1, OP. 88.

VORLAGEN:

1. Die Simrocksche Ausgabe der Partitur.
2. Brahms' Handexemplar der Partitur, im Besitz der Gesellschaft der Musikfreunde in Wien.

BEMERKUNGEN:

Das Quintett erschien im Verlag von N. Simrock in Berlin im Jahre 1883, mit dem Titel: »Quintett für zwei Violinen, zwei Brat-schen und Violoncell von Johannes Brahms. Op. 88.« Verlagsnummer 8314.

Die Partitur ist nahezu fehlerfrei. Im Handexemplar ist bloß ein fehlendes ◁ ▷ im 203. Takt des 2. Satzes in der 1. Violine eingetragen. Im 1. Satz Takt 139 lautet das 3. Viertel der 1. Bratsche , was dem Takt 143 entsprechend richtiggestellt wurde. Ebenso wurde im Takt 108 des 2. Satzes das 4. Achtel der 1. Bratsche, das dis lautete, der Analogie von Takt 24 dieses Satzes entsprechend korrigiert. Ferner war im 87. Takt des Finales ein augenscheinliches Versehen richtigzustellen. Die 1. Bratsche hat im letzten Viertel dieses Taktes den Akkord:

Dieser Akkord ist auf der Bratsche ungreifbar, weshalb die oberste Note beseitigt wurde, die ohnedies, da in der 2. Bratsche enthalten, entbehrlich ist.

QUINTETT NR. 2, OP. 111.

VORLAGEN:

1. Die Simrocksche Partiturausgabe.
2. Brahms' Handexemplar der Partitur, im Besitz der Gesellschaft der Musikfreunde in Wien.

BEMERKUNGEN:

Das Werk erschien im Jahre 1891, mit dem Titel: »Zweites Quintett (G dur) für zwei Violinen, zwei Bratschen und Violoncell von Johannes Brahms. Op. 111.« Verlagsnummer 9508.

Die Partitur ist fast fehlerfrei, das Handexemplar ohne Korrektur.

QUINTETT, OP. 115.

VORLAGEN:

1. Die Simrocksche Partiturausgabe.
2. Die Simrocksche Stimmenausgabe.
3. Brahms' Handexemplar der Partitur, im Besitz der Gesellschaft der Musikfreunde in Wien.
4. Die Original-Handschrift, im Besitz der Gesellschaft der Musikfreunde in Wien.

BEMERKUNGEN:

Das Werk erschien im Jahre 1892 bei N. Simrock in Berlin mit dem Titel: »Quintett für Clarinette (oder Bratsche) 2 Violinen, Bratsche und Violoncell von Johannes Brahms. Op. 115.« Verlagsnummer 9710. Die Partitur ist so gut wie fehlerfrei, einzelne unbedeutende Ungenauigkeiten (Bogen u. dgl.) wurden nach der Stimmenausgabe richtiggestellt. Das Handexemplar enthält eine Korrektur, die hier zu berücksichtigen war: die 5. Variation im Finale (Takt 161) hat in der Originalausgabe die Tempobezeichnung »Con moto«, die in der Coda, bei Takt 193, durch die Bezeichnung »Un poco meno mosso« wieder aufgehoben erscheint. Beide Angaben sind im Handexemplar durchgestrichen, womit die Absicht eines einheitlichen Zeitmaßes für den ganzen Satz (♩ = ♩) klar ausgedrückt ist, und zwar eines Zeitmaßes, das mit dem des 1. Satzes, auf dessen Hauptthema die Coda zurückgreift, genau übereinstimmt.

Die Original-Handschrift trägt zum Schluß das Datum: »Ischl. Sommer 91. J. B.« Bemerkenswert ist eine jedenfalls erst später vorgenommene, in der Handschrift bloß flüchtig skizzierte Änderung und Erweiterung in der Hauptgruppe des 1. Satzes, welche die Wirkung dieser Stelle unvergleichlich hebt. Takt 10 ff. lautet nämlich im Manuskript noch folgendermaßen:

QUARTETT NR. 1 UND 2, OP. 51.

VORLAGEN:

1. Die Partiturausgabe des Verlags N. Simrock in Berlin.
2. Die Stimmenausgabe desselben Verlags.
3. Brahms' Handexemplar der Partitur, im Besitz der Gesellschaft der Musikfreunde in Wien.
4. Die Original-Handschriften beider Quartette, im Besitz der Gesellschaft der Musikfreunde in Wien.

BEMERKUNGEN:

Die Quartette erschienen (in Einzelausgaben) im Jahre 1873 bei N. Simrock mit dem Titel: »Zwei Quartette für 2 Violinen, Bratsche und Violoncell, seinem Freunde Dr. Theodor Billroth in Wien zugeeignet von Johannes Brahms. Op. 51. No. 1. C moll. No. 2. A moll.« Verlagsnummern 7378 und 7379.

Partitur und Stimmen sind fast fehlerfrei. Das Handexemplar des c moll-Quartetts enthält keinerlei Eintragung, das des a moll-Quartetts eine Stichfehlerberichtigung (3. Satz, Takt 173 $\sharp dis$ in der 1. Violine) und eine kleine Änderung in der 1. Violine im 21. und 22. Takt des Finales, die in der Originalausgabe beide folgendermaßen lauteten:

Der Vergleich mit den (undatierten) Original-Handschriften ergab nichts für die Revision Bemerkenswertes.

Wien, im Frühjahr 1927.

QUARTETT NR. 3, OP. 67.

VORLAGEN:

1. Die Simrocksche Partiturausgabe.
2. Die Simrocksche Stimmenausgabe.
3. Brahms' Handexemplar der Partitur, im Besitz der Gesellschaft der Musikfreunde in Wien.
4. Die Original-Handschrift (in Privatbesitz).

BEMERKUNGEN:

Das Quartett erschien im Jahre 1876 bei N. Simrock in Berlin mit dem Titel: »Quartett (in B dur No. 3) für 2 Violinen, Bratsche und Violoncell, seinem Freunde Professor Th. W. Engelmann in Utrecht zugeeignet von Johannes Brahms. Op. 67.« Verlagsnummer 7892.

Partitur- wie Stimmenausgabe sind so gut wie fehlerfrei. Das Handexemplar enthält einige geringfügige Änderungen, die hier berücksichtigt wurden. Die ursprüngliche Lesart ist nachstehend angeführt. Im 2. Satz lautete Takt 36, letztes Viertel, die 1. Violine folgendermaßen:

Ebenso rhythmisiert ist in der Originalausgabe Takt 38—39 die 2. Violine. (Die Änderung macht aus Zweiunddreißigsteltriolen einfache Zweiunddreißigstel.)

Im 3. Satz lautete Takt 103 das letzte Achtel der 1. Violine e anstatt g. In der Coda dieses Satzes lautete Takt 193—194 die Bratsche folgendermaßen:

Die Original-Handschrift zeigt zahlreiche spätere Änderungen, deren interessanteste Takt 172—178 des Finales betrifft. An Stelle dieser neun Takte standen ursprünglich die folgenden:

Hans Gál.

Sextett Nr. 1
für 2 Violinen, 2 Bratschen und 2 Violoncelle

Johannes Brahms, Op. 18
(Veröffentlicht 1862)

343

352

361

Poco più Moderato

Scherzo

Allegro molto

26

Scherzo da capo senza
replica e poi la Coda

J. B. 17

Coda
Più animato

32

425

435

444

Animato, poco a poco più

Sextett Nr. 2

für 2 Violinen, 2 Bratschen und 2 Violoncelle

Johannes Brahms, Op. 36
(Veröffentlicht 1866)

205

217

255

265

E

275

381

393

403

Un poco sostenuto

Scherzo
Allegro non troppo

Presto giocoso

Tempo primo

34(78)

J.B.18

Poco Allegro

D Animato

50 (94)

Quintett Nr. 1
für 2 Violinen, 2 Bratschen und Violoncell

Johannes Brahms, Op. 88
(Veröffentlicht 1883)

Allegretto vivace

Tempo I

Presto

28(122)

Quintett Nr. 2
für 2 Violinen, 2 Bratschen und Violoncell

Johannes Brahms, Op. 111
(Veröffentlicht 1891)

Un poco Allegretto

1. Violine

2. Violine

1. Bratsche

2. Bratsche

Violoncell

Vivace ma non troppo presto

Quintett

für Klarinette (oder Bratsche), 2 Violinen, Bratsche und Violoncell

Johannes Brahms, Op. 115
(Veröffentlicht 1892)

G Quasi sostenuto

Adagio

Presto non assai, ma con sentimento

Quartett Nr. 1
für 2 Violinen, Bratsche und Violoncell

Seinem Freunde D.ʳ Theodor Billroth in Wien zugeeignet

Johannes Brahms, Op. 51 Nr. 1
(Veröffentlicht 1873)

4 (188)

Romanze
Poco Adagio

Allegretto molto moderato e comodo

Allegretto D.C.

24(208)

Quartett Nr. 2
für 2 Violinen, Bratsche und Violoncell

Seinem Freunde Dr. Theodor Billroth in Wien zugeeignet

Johannes Brahms, Op. 51 Nr. 2
(Veröffentlicht 1873)

Allegretto vivace

Tempo di Minuetto

Finale
Allegro non assai

Quartett Nr. 3
für 2 Violinen, Bratsche und Violoncell

Seinem Freunde Professor Th. W. Engelmann in Utrecht zugeeignet

Johannes Brahms, Op. 67
(Veröffentlicht 1876)

Da Capo sin' al ⊕ e poi la Coda

Coda

Poco Allegretto con Variazioni

2da volta rit.

Doppio Movimento